# FATHERING

## A Practical Guide for Dads

# GRACE KETTERMAN, M.D.

Beacon Hill Press of Kansas City
Kansas City, Missouri

Copyright 1997
by Beacon Hill Press of Kansas City

ISBN 083-411-6375

Printed in the
United States of America

Cover Design: Kevin Williamson
Cover Photo: Comstock

"Reflection and Action" sections: Bonnie Perry

All Scripture quotations are from the King James Version unless noted otherwise.

Quotation from the *Modern Language Bible. The New Berkeley Version in Modern English, Revised Version* (MLB). © 1945, 1959, 1969 by Hendrickson Publishers, Inc. Used by permission.

Quotation from *The New Testament in Modern English* (PHILLIPS), Revised Student Edition, by J. B. Phillips, translator. Copyright 1958, 1960, 1972 by J. B. Phillips. Reprinted with the permission of the Macmillan Publishing Company.

**Library of Congress Cataloging-in-Publication Data**
Ketterman, Grace H.
    Fathering : a practical guide for dads / Grace Ketterman.
      p.   cm.
    ISBN 0-8341-1637-5
    1. Fathers—Religious life.   2. Fatherhood—Religious aspects—
Christianity.   I. Title.
    BV4529.K47   1997
    248.8'421—dc21                            97-16707
                                                        CIP

10  9  8  7  6  5  4  3  2  1

# Contents

# Introduction

Few roles in life are as important as being a father, and almost none so difficult.

Let's face some researched facts. In the 44 years between 1950 and 1994, the number of children living in homes where moms were the only parent increased from 6 percent to 24 percent. Some 19 million children in 1994 lived in homes with no father present![1]

The tragic truth is that the absence of fathers does make a difference. For example, fatherless families are 5 times more likely to be poor and 10 times more likely to be extremely poor than those with a father. The kids in these father-absent homes are more likely to experience teenage parenthood, quit school, commit crimes, and experience a number of antisocial problems.[2]

A large Midwest newspaper published research by Ross Parke, a University of California, Riverside, child development specialist. The article reveals that fathers who are regular play partners with their children have kids who can both send and recognize clear emotional signals.[3]

Another researcher this article quotes is psychologist John Snarey from Emory University. He conducted and published a four-decade study of some 250 dads in the Boston area. He found that sons were more successful educationally when their dads stayed involved with them during adolescence. Boys need their fathers' support in their social, emotional, and intellectual development. Daughters, by contrast, were generally more successful when they had their fathers' support for their athletic achievements.[4]

My interpretation of these findings is this: Those areas

of life in which each gender or individual is naturally more successful do not need a lot of support. But in whatever arena a child struggles, he or she needs and thrives on encouragement from a father's strong involvement.

My own experience verifies Dr. Snarey's findings. Despite his own restricted schooling, my father encouraged each of his seven children to gain as much education as possible and to be as successful as we could in the various careers to which God called us. He carefully perused our grade cards and expressed his pride or, at times, his concern. He cared how we did our chores and demanded excellence in all of our performances.

As a result, six of the seven of us had schooling beyond high school. Four of us have college degrees and postcollege studies. Five of us have children who also achieved college degrees and are reasonably well-adjusted people.

A recent book makes a powerful statement about the significance of married fathers: "Married fatherhood is the single most reliable, and relied upon, prescription for socializing males."[5] An even more recent book is by David Popenoe. He states that "the main reason for contemporary father absence is the decline of marriage."[6]

To be—and stay—married and have a decent job with an income above poverty level usually demands a role model. And since the world war of the 1940s, more and more families have lacked a committed male role model. As each new generation has succeeded the last, therefore, there is a decrease in the knowledge about being a good father. Currently there is a resurgence in the quest to restore fatherhood to its position of dignity and importance.

When I was a practicing pediatrician from 1957 to 1963, I became frustrated when by himself a father brought in a sick child. It seemed that dads had an incredible lack of knowledge about their children. Rarely could they give me any significant facts about the child's present illness, they often could not recall the child's birth date, and rarely did they know a medical history. Even then many dads were backing away from healthy family involvement, much less responsibility.

Two factors contributed to this. One, of course, was the loss of so many fathers with the vicissitudes of the war. But the other stemmed from the immense revolution taking place among women. The so-called women's movement had catapulted wives from a posture of submission to one of great control. Moms seemed to be trying to prove they really didn't need help from their spouses. A popular song of those times went, "Anything you can do, I can do better! I can do anything better than you!" Battle lines were drawn; men, already insecure as family members, could not tolerate the berating and criticism of their wives. When a wife would try to tell her spouse how to change a diaper or give a bath, he would easily feel stupid and put down. One husband stated that he felt *despised* by his wife.

A quick and easy solution for many dads was to work harder. It was emotionally far safer for a man to spend long hours on the job where he was successful than to risk failure in a responsibility at home. The lines were drawn. He would stay at work, make a good living, and Mom would take care of the kids.

By the mid-'70s, these lines moved again. Wives were weary of the monotony of household chores and child care. The women's movement beckoned with the glamour of a career. Women were urged to prove to themselves and their "sisters" that they could amount to something and excel over the men. It seemed no one really wanted to stay home with the children. I even heard a man and woman argue over who should miss work to nurse a sick child. It sounded to my sensitive ear as if no one really wanted the child. I have felt immense sadness, but no surprise, at the increases in child crime and teen suicide. When no one *really* wants you, what's the use?

Few parents will admit they don't want their children, though many at times wish they had never had any. But many children with whom I've worked somehow *believe* their parents don't care about them.

So once again, you know why we're creating this series of books on healthy family structuring. And, dads, you can see why an entire book is addressed to you. I hope I have pulled together some information that will enable you to see your immense importance to your families and some common sense guidelines. We want to see you understand your position in the family and fill it with greatness!

# 1

# *Father—a Partner*

Clara and Dan seemed like the ideal couple. They were fun in any group with easy laughter and ready wit. They were popular and always on the guest lists of their friends. But at home there was quite another story. Dan found something wrong about most of Clara's decisions, and tasks about the house rarely pleased him. She felt she was bound to defend herself constantly, and even then she sensed Dan's grave disapproval. Arguments, often outspoken and felt deeply within each, were waged daily. Gradually each withdrew, at home, into separate worlds of silent pain, confusion, and anger, each wanting his or her own way. Even when one accomplished winning, there was a price to pay—the loss of a sense of partnering and closeness.

One answer to the power struggles between men and women is the creation of a true partnership. In an incredibly concise manner, God revealed how He created Eve for Adam. It took only four verses in Gen. 2:21-24 to tell the story. God anesthetized Adam, removed one of his ribs, and from it made a helpmeet for him. God did not ask Adam to be Eve's boss!

Some wedding vows include this story with the symbols of the rib being taken from Adam's side, not his head or foot. Eve was designated a partner, not his servant nor his boss.

It was such a partnership that I witnessed between my parents. Farm people had to function as partners. My mother took care of the chickens, the gardens, and often helped my father with livestock and other work. Dad, in turn, helped carry heavy buckets of water to heat for our huge amount of laundry or to water the gardens. During the years of our mother's poor health, he could do the laundry, help clean house, and cook or bake delicious food when the need arose. No task was too effeminate for him if it needed doing or when we girls were in school.

Never did I hear Dad criticized for being a sissy or for doing "women's work." I can recall the kindness with which he established care for our mom during her many illnesses. Together they set rules for us, their children, and consistently they held to them. We learned the values of honoring each other, being gentle, loving, funny, and mutually helpful from these partners. Having and raising children, gardens, farm crops, and animals were no small challenges then or now. But doing it together made it possible—even enjoyable.

"So how can we be or become partners in the 1990s?" I can hear you ask. Let me tell you.

## Managing Your Home

In every household there are decisions, plans, and jobs that are required. Perhaps he likes dark colors for a bedspread and drapes. She, of course, prefers rose and just a touch of blue. How can they resolve even such a concrete decision as a color theme in decorating their first home?

*He* thinks he is supposed to be the head of the house. To him that means he's the boss, and she should submit to him. That's scriptural, of course. But he forgot he is equally ordered to love his wife as Christ loves the Church.

Now let's think about how Jesus loved that Church. First, He exemplified how to live and serve. Then He carried the process so far He willingly died for it. True, He chastised the phony Pharisees and did a few choice things to those who desecrated the Temple. But they weren't members of His family, the Church. My paraphrase of Christ's model would be something like this. "My beloved wife, I'm so proud of your great skills. Your appearance is always lovely, so I suspect you know how to create a harmonious home. I have to paint the outside of this home, so I'll trust you to decorate the inside. Let's plan together the colors and designs that will give us a house we can turn into a home." Could any wife be less than excited about such a husband? I suspect she'd find a way to include his special colors in a corner someplace.

A mentor of mine described the true meaning of a head of the house. He is like the leader of a clan in days of old. It was his privilege to attend to the needs of every member of that group. Only when all of them were safe, fed, and had their needs met would this noble man sit down to eat and consider his own needs. Such a man was my father. When every chore possible was done and the household was in order, he would sit in his rocking chair. The brightest lamps were allocated to those of us who were students, so he would sit close to the dim kerosene lamp and laboriously read until he fell asleep. I can never recall his being impatient if one of us awakened him with a need or problem. If he did not have the solution, he would find it. He was so confident I cannot recall ever doubting that he had the right answers.

Meanwhile, Mom would check our spelling words, hear us read aloud, or copy our scribbles into her excellent penmanship. Translated, these examples state that a partner dad is one who is there—wherever his family needs him—and that he and Mom share the responsibilities and privileges of teaching basic responsibilities, building a sense of significance, and nurturing their youngsters. When one's tasks are done, he checks with the other about those still incomplete.

## Managing the Children

Hank had found the answers to getting his way. He realized early in life that his mom adored him. He discovered how to look at her, make her laugh, and give her adoring hugs. Much of his behavior was sincere, but more than a little was designed to make her give in to his every whim. And she did.

Hank's dad caught on to his manipulation and tried to set limits to correct the deceitfulness that was corrupting his son's soul. But Mom, caught right in the center of Hank's web, took sides against her husband. She had a most difficult task extricating herself from the triangle Hank had so intricately created. In fact, Hank was well on his way to serious problems in the community because he had grown to be so powerful, he could influence friends to get into trouble.

Hank's help arrived none too soon, when both parents finally recognized the depth of his problems. Mom realized she had been indulging and enabling her son to get his way. She saw his rudeness to his father and other authorities and finally experienced his disdain for her when she eventually tried to restrict him. When both parents established a partnership, their combined strength brought Hank's behaviors under control and began to rebuild healthy relationships among all of the family members.

All kids want their way. When they discover weak areas in parental partnering, they will always try to escape from healthy boundaries to total freedom, even though they are not ready for it. Wise fathers work out problems with their wives in order to maintain strong protection until their children are well prepared for more freedom.

Here are some how-tos for husbands.

1. Find time every day to spend with your wife. Use this time to show her love and respect as a person. Share with her and listen to her.
2. Together formulate a set of goals for your family, including marital as well as child-rearing ones. What sort of persons do you want your children to be at age 23? How can both of you help those qualities grow in your children now?
3. Discuss together the basic rules it will take to reach the goals you have set. Such policies as requiring respect and kindness, no hurting of each other, and working together as a unit will prevent the triangular web Hank and his mom were spinning with Dad.
4. Review daily the way things are working. Usually consequences for breaking rules have to be adjusted. Rules must be consistently enforced, yet flexible enough to meet changing situations. You must stick together as parents to prevent the breakdown of your system.
5. Check out the climate of your home. Is it mainly warm, friendly, and conducive to creativity? Be sure it does not become harsh, cold, and rejecting.
6. Is your relationship as spouses setting a good example for your children? Will your marriage enable them to make wise choices for a spouse and help them form a strong marriage later?

If you can make these suggestions conform to your personalities and situations, you can resolve almost all problems.

## Managing Your Money

"I don't have enough money for groceries," Ellen mourned, "but Len always finds money for new golf equipment!" Len's slant was this: "I work hard more than 60 hours most weeks. I deserve a little reward and fun for all my efforts!"

Ellen and Len, typical of so many couples, are enemies instead of partners when it comes to budgeting. Having grown up with relative affluence has ill prepared young parents for the stringent demands of today's uncertain economy. Their parents lived through the tension of the postwar era and vowed they'd make life easier for their children. In many cases it was too easy, and for these young parents to recognize the need to deprive themselves of some things was unbearable. So couples have pretended their way to luxury via credit cards. They have fallen in power struggles through battling over who spends the most.

How useful it is to spend that daily time together to solve the money problem. There's no need for anger and rivalry over who gets to have the most money. Partners decide together about financial needs, and they prioritize those categories. They both are willing to give up a bit of their own spending in order to successfully operate the business of managing their family financially.

Living within the established budget can be a major challenge. Dads need to be careful to avoid guilt if they can't afford luxuries. They must be honest with their wives about needing help and support, not blame or criticism. Of course, wives need the assurances that Dad is not siphoning off money for expensive hobbies or needless spending.

You can see how vital this partnership concept is. You can also see that it demands openness and accurate information. It takes the willingness to respect each other's feelings and needs. It requires each one to be clear about the distinction between facts and feelings. For example, you may feel your spouse doesn't love you if he or she has to say, "We can't go out to dinner this week because we've used up our entertainment budget for the month." The fact is, the money's gone. We agreed to abide by the budgetary rules. We'll go after next payday. The facts are clear. Love is committed. We can't always do what we'd like to do. End of problem.

In the first book of this series, *Marriage: First Things First,* one topic we discussed was maturity. Mature individuals can postpone present pleasure for the future good. You can see how vitally important that concept is in living harmoniously as partners. Each must give in sometimes, and yet each must be sensitive to the other.

In managing money, parents must stand together for their children. In this desire to please their children and "make them happy," most parents probably give them too much money and too many things. Children need only a few things and often have more fun digging in the dirt and building with twigs than they do with expensive toys. They also learn to be creative by improvising. So once again parental partners must stand together in teaching values, allowing children to earn some of their money and to work for a few special toys. By doing so, children will value and appreciate the items they have and are more likely to care for them.

There are many good books on how to manage money well. Find the time to read them and sift out ideas. Then put the principles to work for your family's security. Do this together. You are partners.

## Rules for Successful Partnership

Small businesses and large corporations may rise or fall, depending on their success at team building and partnering. So do families. Here are some simple and difficult rules to help you rise and shine as a successful Christian family.

1. Keep sacred enough time to communicate; let nothing interfere.
2. Keep your mind open to what is best, not who is right.
3. Be honest and open about fácts, and acquire from every possible source all the information you can about each issue that arises. (Within reason!)
4. Be equally honest about your feelings, but bal-

ance them with facts. For example, "I feel tense when you are so stern with the children. I'm afraid you'll push them to be rebellious." Fact is, my parents were too strict, and I nearly rebelled. My father was a good balance for my mother's being too hard on us. He saved the day for me.

5. Be careful to listen well. This means you hear your partner's ideas, read his or her emotions, care about both, and compare them with how you feel and what you think. Discuss any differences thoughtfully and kindly—not bent on getting your own way.

6. When your spouse's desires simply cannot be granted, wish with him or her that they could!

7. Learn how to debate by sticking to the topic at hand, presenting a wise point of view but being willing to modify that when valid new facts are discovered.

8. Negotiating works through any disagreement. To negotiate, you must balance giving in with holding out when that provides the greatest benefit.

9. Be willing to admit mistakes, and avoid implying, "I told you so!" Apologies are healing.

10. Review past actions and decisions. Learn from them. If they worked, use them often, and strive to improve on them. If they failed, search out why they didn't work, and avoid repeating the same mistakes.

11. Take time out to play a game of Scrabble (or whatever is fun for you both!).

# Reflection and Action

1. List three tasks in which you and your wife partner well. Next, each of you list three tasks in which you believe partnering skills could be improved. Discuss practical steps to make the desired improvements.

We partner well in:

*a.*

*b.*

*c.*

He thinks we could partner better in:

*a.*

*b.*

*c.*

She thinks we could partner better in:

*a.*

*b.*

*c.*

2. Share with your spouse what you remember of your own parents' partnering skills.

3. List five character qualities you want your children to exhibit at age 23. Of these qualities, check those they are well on their

way to achieving. Which need some extra work? List three ways you can encourage your child in these areas.

_____

_____

_____

_____

_____

_____

_____

_____

_____

_____

4. When was the last time you made a verbal apology to your spouse? Were the children present? If this is an area you need to work on, write a short prayer of commitment._____

_____

_____

_____

# 2

## Father—a Teacher

"Oh, goody!" my mind chattered. "What do I get to see this time?" It was a gorgeous May morning. The sun was warm but not hot. The lilacs and yellow roses bloomed and scented the farm air with subtle delight. I was not yet in school, so I was totally and exuberantly free.

My father was a man of few words but many expressions, an unusually gifted teacher about life. This morning, as he often did, he came to the house from the farmyard. Catching my eye, he winked, looked toward the back door, and crooked his index finger. Instantly I saw in the twinkle of his brown eyes a glimpse of an awesome new experience.

Dad held my five-year-old hand in his big, rough, tanned one, and I skipped along beside him. Sometimes this sort of experience led to a visit to a squealing litter of pink new piglets. Often there was a soft new baby calf or an impossibly wobbly baby colt barely able to stand on his spindly long legs.

But today our path led to the chicken house. I was used to seeing the fluffy balls of soft fur that were baby chicks. I could pick one up at the risk of an angry peck from its protective mother hen and hold it against my cheek. Words couldn't express the ecstasy of the feel, the sight, and the sound of such a simple event.

The experience this lovely May morning held, however,

was a new one. Dad had discovered a baby chick that was in the process of being hatched, and he knew I would be breathlessly excited to see this process. Indeed, I was. I literally held my breath as I watched the egg. It vibrated as the chick inside busily chipped away at the brittle shell. Finally pieces of that shell fell off, exposing the baby. To my childish surprise, the chick was not yellow and fluffy but wet, big-eyed, and horrible! It would peck vigorously for a while and then rest for a time. Again it would peck and rest. At one point, the rest time became so long, I was fearful. Instinctively, I reached out to remove the shell and set free the ugly creature inside.

Ever so gently, I felt Dad's hand restraining mine. I heard his voice softly explaining that God had made a plan for chicks to be hatched. They needed to rest and work to get out of their shell because that process made them strong and taught them how to breathe. Only through this laborious struggle could the chick survive outside its protective shell. I knew if God had planned it that way, and Daddy had explained it, that's the way it was. So I withdrew my hand and, in silent wonder, watched the rest of the procedure.

In the eternity of childhood minutes, the baby was free. In the warm sun, its wet, ugly hairs became the familiar ball of fluff I recognized. I had witnessed a miracle, and my childish mind was enriched.

My father was a farmer with only eight years of formal education. Yet he was a master teacher. Few dads today can share with a child the wonders of nature that were common to us on an old-fashioned farm. But the basic principles of this story remain unchanged.

1. Be alert to the everyday events that do occur in your home and neighborhood. A bird's nest observed from a safe distance will do. A lift to Dad's shoulder and the establishment of silence to avoid frightening the mother bird will teach consideration of God's creatures, and it reveals the wonder of that mother's care of her nestlings. A litter of kit-

tens or puppies or even the slow, silent opening of the petals of a rosebud can teach lessons.

2. Set up some events of your own. Seeds planted in dirt in a glass jar show how roots and stems alike come from a barely visible beginning. Observing the growth of moss and even molds can reveal God's creative power. (If your kitchen is like mine, mold is not hard to find!)

3. Use any and all occasions possible to affirm God's wisdom. He has a purpose, a reason, for everything. One of our tasks lies in discovering what that is. By focusing with a child, he or she will learn to be curious. Curiosity is the taproot of learning. Finding out God's purpose for nature can help a child think about His purpose for him or her. Children with no sense of meaning or purpose for their lives are at risk; your teaching can minimize that risk!

4. Teach each child, at times, individually. I suspect my baby chick lesson would have been much less memorable had I been one of several children observing the event. There has to be a balance in individual versus family groups. But if as a dad you understand the importance of it, you can probably find bits of time for both.

5. Remember it's not convenient to take time out from a busy, often frantic, schedule to teach a child. It is, however, a practice you will not regret. In fact, your joy in teaching an excited child will greatly reward your efforts. My son-in-law not only plants seeds with his sons but also has them help him transplant them in the spring to flower beds outside. Every visitor learns of the part these children play in beautifying their home.

## Teaching Across Generations

One of my favorite pastimes as a child was listening

to stories. Those I liked best were the experiences of my parents as children and their memories of my grandparents. The stories I loved best were personal ones. My father, for example, described trying to get a drink from the water pump one bitterly cold winter's day. He had pumped a pipe full of cold water. As he bent to catch the water in his hand from the pipe and lap it up, he found his tongue had frozen to the heavy iron pipe. No one heard his cries for help, and he was too frightened to wait. Finally he pulled his tongue free and was horrified to see a tiny piece of it frozen to the pipe. He healed, but he could still show me the little scar that verified the story.

I learned from Dad about his father's frightening trek across the continent from Pennsylvania to Ohio and finally to the plains of central Kansas. The stories of blizzards seemed impossible, but I read about them later in books. My grandfather had lived through them, and my own father later survived more of them. Plagues of insects occasionally destroyed crops, leaving families destitute until a new season arrived. Hail, drought, dust storms, and epidemics assailed those early pioneers. But my lesson was this: they never gave up. They teamed up. With each other and with other families, they helped, shared, and survived. So, I discovered, could I.

It took time to tell these stories, to teach the many lessons they contained. I'm certain Dad wanted to relax, to read, to fall asleep in the evenings. But he rarely did. Instead, he talked with us, read to us, joked and played with us. He taught us about life.

## Teaching About Values

Going to town was a big event when I was 10. If he had time, Dad would often ask, "Anybody want to ride along?" My sisters would be involved with their own stuff, but I had learned going anywhere with Dad could involve an adventure. I loved being with Dad and seeing people.

So on this occasion off we went, seven long miles in the old Model A Ford. At the end of several errands, Dad entered one of the savings and loan institutions of our town. He gave the manager a tidy sum of $5. That's pocket money now, but it was a lot of money on the edge of the big depression of the early '30s.

As we walked back to our car, Dad honored me with a major confidence. I've not yet decided if the bigger lesson was that it was his story or the fact that he trusted me as if I were an adult by sharing it with me.

The manager of that financial institution had insisted that my father owed him $5. He had billed him, caught him on the streets and pestered him, and had even called him repeatedly to get his money. My father was an honest and conscientious man. Furthermore, he kept daily, accurate accounts of every penny he owed or spent. He was certain he did not owe anyone $5.

Over time, however, Dad began to include his witness as a man of God into his deliberations about that dreadful $5. Finally, he told me, he decided the manager really believed it was owed to him. And it seemed a bit of a Christian testimony to accede the battle to the other man. He paid $5, which was a sacrifice to him and which he knew he did not owe, to say to an unbeliever, "I'd rather give this to you for the glory of God than to keep it and have you discredit Him or me."

You can see the lesson that Dad taught me in going the limit to live out his faith and be a testimony to one man. I'm 60 years older now than then, yet that lesson is indelibly printed in my mind. Dad taught me how to give in at times, even when I know I'm right, for the sake of living out the gospel.

How are you teaching your children? Are you willing to be transparent, to share with them some of your life? If so, you can give them a pattern to live by, a way of life that is not the easy one, but the path that will glorify God.

The way a father teaches values and priorities is so important we'll discuss more about these areas later.

## How to Teach

I'd like to think these examples of my father portray methods for teaching as well as content. But let's summarize specific ways in which, know it or not, you do teach.

1. *Taking time* says to a child, "You are important to me—more important than my work, my hobbies, my rest." It also says, "I have something valuable to share with you—it's more fun shared with you!" Great self-esteem comes from such fatherly (or motherly) teaching.

2. *Showing respect* in teaching lifts a child to a level almost equal to Dad's. When a child feels Dad's respect, it is much more likely he or she will return such a courtesy—and that he or she will give respect and trust to the Heavenly Father.

3. *Being an example* of the idea taught makes it understandable. It validates the concept and enables the child to copy it, to try it out. If it's worthwhile, the child will probably weave it into his or her own person.

4. *Teaching with love* says that this child and this teachable moment are precious to me, the father. Because I love you, I crave being with you; I want to pass on to you those experiences that are meaningful to me.

5. *Teaching through action.* My father could have explained to me for an hour how miraculous is the hatching of a baby chick. From start to finish of that memorable few minutes he said hardly two dozen words. His gestures, his touch, his own interest spoke volumes to my mind.

6. A saint of old, Francis of Assisi, said, "Preach Christ; and if you must, use words." There are

times, fathers, when you, too, must *use words.* Keep them few, and conceive of them as the precious, distilled, concentrated drops of God's wisdom. Say them gently, and watch your child's face to ascertain his or her comprehension.

Convey consistently your honesty, your own curiosity, and your love of learning. Be an explorer of your beliefs, the world about you, and your child's mind. Seek to saturate your and your family's beings with emotional richness, intellectual stimulation, and above all, spiritual life and reality. As you teach and live what you convey, you will be rewarded with watching your family bond in a love nothing else can match.

## Reflection and Action

1. With your spouse, discuss ways that the skill of teaching was or was not modeled in your childhood home.

2. List three times during the week you could spend an additional 15 minutes with your children. _____

_____

_____

3. List the five most important principles you want your children to learn from observing your life. Grade yourself in each area: A, B, C, or D. (The fact that you're reading this book indicates you don't deserve an F!)

_____

_____

_____

_____

_____

4. Together with your children, name 10 intellectually enriching activities that your family could enjoy together (e.g., visit the museum, zoo, planetarium; take a nature walk and identify birds or animals along the way; read classic storybooks before bedtime). Next, choose 2 or 3 of these activities to do in the coming month.

_____    _____

_____    _____

_____    _____

_____    _____

_____    _____

5. Schedule a time to talk to each of your children about school, but _not_ about their grades. Open the conversation by asking questions like, "Tell me why science is your favorite subject in school," or "What subjects are you studying now that you might like to learn more about?" or "What is the most interesting thing you learned in school last week?" View this conversation as a time to get to know your child as an individual.

# 3

## *Father—a Protector*

The clouds were nearly black, threatening the spawning of a twister so dreaded on our Kansas summertime plains. Lightning darted and thunder rumbled. Then it happened. Far to the north of home, so small and frail beneath the storm's magnitude, appeared a funnel cloud. There grew a frightening stillness, the blackness turned to a sickening green, and the imminent threat of a tornado striking our farm was undeniable.

Firmly, Dad moved the family to the shelter of our basement. But he stood on the back porch, watching the speed and direction of the approach of disaster. At that time I was unaware of it, but I know now he silently sought the Heavenly Father's protection.

With an old broom, Dad swept the pelting rain off the porch as his eyes focused on that ominous cloud. I think he knew I was there, carefully hidden behind his strong body and that broom. I knew I should be stowed safely away in that cellar with Mom, but I somehow knew I was better off with my father. Miraculously, the funnel receded into the clouds, and we were spared a disaster. My Heavenly Father is my Protector, as my dad once was. How easy he made it to trust Him!

The likeness of my dad to God the Father was obvious to me. I believe, in fact, that is exactly the way God planned things. When dads follow God and walk closely with Him, their footprints design the path their children should follow to find Him. Some dads do this well; others leave a crooked path with wandering detours that dangerously risk the child getting lost.

Dads may well need to protect their families from nature's storms even today. The children I know feel best if Dad is there with them during any upheaval of nature. But the more dangerous storms we face in the '90s are those involving different risks.

## Violence

In many large cities crime is a daily fear producer. Most kids who grow up in an area of poverty, drug abuse, and broken homes have known someone who was murdered. They have often seen shootings and witnessed fights among people in their own homes. They have little if any security; no place of safety exists for them.

The violence of any community becomes excitement for the media. Radios blare the tragedies of human life for everyone to hear, and TV explicitly bares it for all eyes to see.

Fathers must learn how to protect their children from becoming calloused, uncaring about the pain of others. And dads must find ways to reach into crime-rife areas, teaching parents there how to offer protection to their children. Several nationwide groups have arisen that provide leadership in such community efforts. If dads take time to volunteer for these opportunities, they can make a difference in the area of violence.

Fathers can also work against violence at home. Let's look at some ways you can do so.

1. *Demonstrate self-control.* For many years our culture has advocated free expression of whatever one feels. Many men seem to feel that they have a

right to explode their anger and act out their aggression in any way they choose. Abuse of women and children by such men has become a regular drama of real life on TV. Godly men must not give in to such behavior. If you have a conflict with your wife, settle it with patience and wisdom. When you must correct your children, do so firmly and gently. Remember: *real* strength is always gentle, and true gentleness is strong.

2. *Do not allow hurting between family members.* Everyone is born with more or less aggressiveness. Children will fight over toys, privileges, and responsibilities. Parents will struggle over control issues. It is easy in such conflicts to physically and verbally abuse one another. Dads, you must help prevent cruelty at home. Form a united team with your wife. Together stop family abuse and work out problem-solving techniques.

3. *Protect your child from hurting himself or herself.* Some children are born with intense emotions. They react dramatically to life's daily events. Even their bodies react intensely to stress. Moms become weary of dealing with such intensity all day. When you are there, help her out, and do your child a favor. Teach children to calm themselves, and help Mom find ways to learn self-control. Here are some ways:

   a. Touch the child gently and firmly, get good eye contact, and verbally tell (don't ask) him or her what to do. The child may need to stop yelling, quit hitting, and go to a quiet place to think.

   b. If he or she fails to obey in a reasonable time, you will have to go to plan B. In this plan you physically restrain your child's violent action. Hold him or her physically until he or she regains control. Take the child to the place where he or she may, for example, have been required to do a task. Stand with the child until the task is completed.

c. To accomplish *b* above: When fights or arguments do arise, stop them. Turn arguments into problem solving. Define the situation clearly, list possible options for solving problems, consider the consequences of each option, and help the child make a good choice. Consistently following through with such a routine can eliminate most fights. It works, by the way, for adults too!

d. Teach anger control to your children. I have learned that denying or hiding anger only seems to make matters worse. Here are the steps to protecting your child from his or her own rage. Teach how to put it into words. "I feel cross," "I'm angry," "I'm furious" are some examples of verbalizing how *I* feel. Next, help him or her discover why the anger is there. A boy might say, "I'm mad because Jill took my ball and bat and went to play with her friends." Finally, help him decide what *he* can do about the problem, not how he can make *her* change. He may, for example, put his equipment away so Jill does not have easy access to it.

Such a plan validates any natural feeling, teaches how to solve most any problem, and gets the child's intellect in control. Instead of allowing the feelings to erupt in possibly disastrous ways, issues are the focus, thoughtful handling of emotions is learned, and habits for a lifetime of successful conflict resolution are mastered.

Now let's look at teaching your child to cope with violence from others. At all ages, your child will confront aggression from other kids. Toddlers bite, kick, and hit other children, often for no known reason. Preschoolers regularly fight for control of a toy or a turn in a game. School-age children fight more subtly for a place in a group or for power of some sort.

A student I once knew was persistently knuckled by a bully sitting next to him in a class. His parents urged him to ignore the boy, thinking that would make the fellow stop. They may also have feared the opponent would become even more violent outside of school if their son reacted to him.

After several months, however, the pain was inflicted just as badly as ever. My young friend's arm was black-and-blue from the torturing blows of his classmate's bent finger into his now tender arm. Somehow the teacher never caught the bully.

At last the boy's father suggested he firmly apply the same blow to his attacker. With a gleam in his eye, my friend awaited his chance. Sure enough, the next day the painful hit landed on his hurting arm. When the teacher looked away, Sam, well taught by now, applied a smarting blow on the arm of his torture master. A look of total surprise and profound pain fixed itself on the face of that bully. Sam gained self-respect, freedom from further hitting, and eventually the respect of the other students who saw him tolerating abuse out of weakness.

Self-defense must be considered carefully in order to prevent a vicious cycle of attack and counterattack. But in today's climate of violence I believe all children need to learn some basic self-protection skills. Many communities offer classes that teach protective measures. Good judgment as well as physical skills is crucial. If a possible bully attack seems likely, it may be wise to run fast to a teacher, a block mother's house, or a hiding place. Help your child memorize safe places and decide what the best chance of protection may be.

Please do not overreact. Dads, you are the ones who must thoughtfully evaluate your neighborhood. How dangerous is it? Are there enough safety factors to reasonably protect your kids? Are your children capable of adequate self-protection? Have you taught them all you can about avoiding fights, getting help, running away, or safely fighting it out? If you feel your family is reasonably safe, you are blessed.

If, however, you find yourself in a community turned violent, you may need to move. I recognize that is not always possible, but make it an option. If you can't move, do whatever is possible to mechanically protect your family. Erecting a fence, installing electronic safety devices, and getting a dog trained to react to strangers are all suggestions from police departments.

These suggestions for providing protection are practical. You may have thought of them already—or even put them into effect. But you may not have considered their symbolism.

As a child, the last sound I recall before falling asleep was a series of clicks. That sound told me Dad had locked all the doors. It said to me that I was safe because Dad had taken the trouble to secure the house. I now know how simple it would have been for any really serious intruder to get in if he'd wanted to. But my father's attempts at protection symbolized safety. It was and has been easy for me to know I'm safe in my Heavenly Father's care. Your protection is not just physical or even emotional in the here and now. It also teaches protection in God for eternity.

Providing adequate protection for your children requires knowing *where* they are and with *whom* they are. Currently my local news channels are creating headlines about good kids joining bad gangs. Some of this trend is because kids seek excitement and adventure. Some comes from gang members who cunningly craft enticements to kids to join them. But some is because fathers don't spend enough time with their children.

Protect your sons and daughters from gangs by:

1. *Offering them time with you*—time to explore, play, work, think, and talk.
2. *Making that time memorable.* The quality of your interactions can be so positive, your kids would have no interest in negative peers. Include laughter, tears, openness about yourself with them. They will crave more!
3. *Helping them discern positive traits from negative.* By careful questioning, you can help them find for themselves the risky or really destructive qualities of bad friends. If you lecture them or criticize their unfavorable friends, you are likely to find your kids defying you and defending their so-called friends. Now there will probably come a point at which you must forbid a truly bad friendship. Kids can be conned. They haven't the wisdom of experience. If you have built a loving, protective bond with your kids, they will accept an occasional definite, immovable boundary setting.
4. *If you do not know, finding out about gangs.* Learn how they operate, seducing both boys and girls to work with them to get money, drugs, and sex. Find out how they bribe, coerce, and finally terrorize kids into submitting to their evil control. Remind your kids that you will always find a way to protect them from even such powerful evil.

## Protection from Agnosticism

Many self-help programs such as Alcoholics Anonymous (AA) are built upon a belief in a Higher Power. There is, however, a major secular influence in our world today that attempts to derogate even generic faith. Dads, you can help to weaken such an influence in the life of your child. Here's how.

1. *Live a life of faith.* Teach God's Word. I will never forget a sight I discovered as a child. One hot summer night I awoke, thirsty. It was a moonlit night, so I padded downstairs to the kitchen for a drink of refreshing water. Nearly at my destination, I heard a sound—a soft but pained moan. Silently I peered into the kitchen. There I saw my father—my incredibly strong dad—kneeling by the yellow chair, silhouetted in the moonlight. Without audible words, I knew he was crying out his worries and sharing his burdens with God. Somehow I knew God was right there; and if my dad needed Him, so would I. My physical thirst was not satisfied that night, but my spiritual thirst was aroused. Once again, Dad's life taught faith to me, a child.

2. *Teach the answers to prayers.* Sometimes your fatherly answer to your child's pleadings must be, "No. That would not be good for you." Weak parents give in to children's demands too often, indulging them and teaching them how to manipulate to get their way. God often must say no to us. We can help our children see denials as loving protection instead of cruelty. When God answers your prayers positively, share those responses with your children. A friend of mine had a near-fatal accident on her way to work. Still trembling with her fear, she told about God's watching over her. Sometimes we fail to see His care and allow ourselves to believe in luck or coincidence. For God's children there is no such thing. His loving protection is promised to us. As we are aware of Him and see His hand throughout our lives, we will recognize how great He is. Such events and thoughts need to be shared with our loved ones so they can also see His love.

3. *Teach your family to pray.* So many dads these

days become extremely busy. They work long hours and exhaust themselves. I truly believe God can help you budget both your time and money so you will have time for your children. A time of prayer as you tuck them into bed provides a great sense of safety and peace to them. Guide them to pray about any mistakes or sins of their day. Help them accept God's forgiveness and yours. Thank God for His promises about taking care of them. Listen to and at times make suggestions for their prayers. Feel with them the stability God will build in their hearts and minds—and yours!

As a result of some three decades of permissive parenting, some of you dads may find it too easy to give in to children's pesterings and demands. It's certainly tempting to take the easy way out. You may, for example, do their assignments for them to rescue them from hurtful consequences. Be alert to these dangers. Either rescuing or giving in will give them a nonverbal message that says, "If you persist, you can always get your way." Equally damaging is the idea that if a job's very hard, someone else will take it over. You can't do really difficult tasks. So many young people are dropping out of life, often because they have come to believe they *can't* do it.

When your child faces a challenge, help him or her get through it, but don't rescue the child from it. Firmly and persistently, require him or her to complete the job. Even when you know you deserve the kudos for your efforts, give them to the child. Kids glow when a dad says, "Jennie, I know you hated cleaning your room. I literally had to drag you through it. But you did it! It looks great. And you bent your will to obey me in the process. I'm proud of you!" Next time it's bound to be just a bit easier. By such a method you will protect your child from finding the easy path and becoming a slob.

Once you build your confidence and overcome your

fears of failure in fathering, you will become excited about being a protective father.

## Reflection and Action

1. Think of a time when you believe God was protecting you from harm. Write about your thoughts and feelings during that time._____

_____

_____

2. Place yourself on the continuum below. Ask your spouse to do the same. Next, list three areas in which you could improve your ability to exercise self-control (e.g., watching television, raising your voice, spending money, etc.).

I exercise extreme                         I have no meaningful
self-control at home                       self-control at home

├──────────────────────────────────────────────────┤

_____        _____

_____        _____

_____        _____

3. Describe your strategy for stopping arguments between your children. Your spouse's strategy. Identify the strengths and weaknesses in both plans. _____

_____

_____

_____

_____

_____

_____

4. Meet with each of your children individually. Ask them what they are most afraid of. Be sensitive as you listen to their answers. Discuss ways they could feel more protected from the things they fear. Develop an action plan together.

5. Describe your personal relationship with God. What is one thing you can do this week that will enrich that relationship?

_____

_____

_____

6. Share your experience of God's help with your children.

# 4

## *Father—a Playfellow*

Even now I cannot always distinguish. Did I have more fun working with Dad or playing with him? He could make the worst of tasks take on an edge of fun by his never failing sense of humor. He could ferret out a funny word or humorous event and, without ridicule, make of it a joke we cherished over time. Frequently he would take out just a minute for play during work. Always he could make a friendly, welcome environment when I was with him. I suspect each of the seven of us kids believed we were his favorite child.

### Play in Action

When I was about five, I recall going everywhere with Dad—in the car, on the wagon, walking, or on the old green John Deere tractor. Invariably at the end of a ride, he would alight from the tractor or wagon, asking me to wait a minute. Then with a happy twinkle in his brown eyes, he would invite, "Jump to me, Gracie!" His strong arms reached up to me, and with perfect confidence I would leap into their safe grasp. He never let me fall. I knew I was safe in him.

Later, it was a logical leap of faith into a loving relationship with my Heavenly Father. He, too, has never let me down.

Some decades later, I was learning psychiatry. One of my patients was a charming girl of 12. She was deeply depressed and found her family very difficult to tolerate at times. One day she told me this story. Her father was a muscular man, and she admired his strength. His favorite game was to sit in front of a rough stucco wall in their kitchen. He would spread out his legs, hold out his arms, and say, "Run to me, Mary Ann!" She would run as fast as her chubby legs could carry her. He would catch her, toss her into the air, and hug her. What fun!

But sometimes this dad would adroitly lean aside as Mary Ann ran. She would crash into the rough wall, smashing her little face as he laughed at her. It did not take a genius to understand this child's sadness. In her world there was little safety, no consistency. Too often, any laughter was at her expense.

Dad, children must never be ridiculed, needlessly hurt, or abused. They thrive only in a climate of unconditional love, approval, and predictability. Perhaps you grew up with those blessings; then again, perhaps you don't have a pattern for providing them for your children. I hope these word pictures with their clear contrasts will help you better understand how important your role as father is.

Let me suggest a few other kinds of play. Long before I heard of the card game of authors, my family played Bible authors. It was a homemade game created by our mother. In her exquisite penmanship, she carefully wrote the name of every book of the Bible on small bits of cardboard, 4 copies of each of the 66 books. All 264 cards were placed in a box and carefully mixed up.

On long winter evenings, Dad popped a dishpan full of our own, homegrown popcorn in a heavy iron skillet. The entire family sat around our biggest dining table and played Bible authors, just as many families now play plain authors. As they grew older, my teenage brothers were a bit bored by this, I could tell; but Dad and Mom believed we needed some fun times together. And I must say the excitement of recalling who had which books and with whom we could trade soon caught even the most sophisticated brother into the fun of it.

It would have been impossible for Mom alone to create such a memorable evening of pure play. Together they pulled it off. Remember the importance of partnering? I suspect it was Dad's marvelous humor and his popcorn that really enticed us into a family fun time.

At Christmastime our big family could eat a ton of treats. During the depression we certainly could not buy cookies or candy. And it was such fun to make them with both Mom and Dad. We had, of course, no electricity in our house. We had no kitchen equipment, which now simplifies cooking. So Mother collected and carefully measured the ingredients for endless batches of cookies and candy. For Dad's powerful arms, mixing the stiff dough was apparently easy. After baking, the cookies and candies were carefully wrapped in waxed paper and packed into boxes. Stored in a very cold room, the goodies awaited the days immediately adjacent to Christmas Day on the big bank calendar.

Intuitively, Dad could tell when each of us had reached the limit of his or her capacity for waiting. A crook of his finger and twinkle of his eye would tell me it was time. He found a way for just the two of us to enter the cold room. But I cannot recall the cold for feeling the warmth of my excitement. Dad teased me by pretending to have trouble untying the string that protected the box. At last it was open! There was an enticing rustle of paper and a slow reach for one delicious cookie. What a treat! It never occurred to me to ask for more. My boundaries were firm. But who could ask for any more? A father who loved and understood me, who took the time to play with me, tease me, and surprise me was priceless.

I hope you have seen the elements of this sort of

play—compassion, finding an exact time, creating suspense, excitement, and, at last, gratification. These are the ingredients of blue ribbon fathering that make traditions and memories have lifetime meaning. I must add that somehow Dad found the opportunities and time to do such fun things with *seven* of us.

## Fun Even in Mistakes

My father was not all fun and games! He was often stern in his disciplines, but he was remarkably fair. He knew when we were being irresponsible, lazy, or careless. But he also knew if a problem arose that was beyond our control.

One day I was ironing a new synthetic fabric blouse. I did not realize this fabric demanded a fairly cool iron. As I set down a hot iron, expecting to make this lovely item look new, I discovered the facts. The iron did not glide over the satin. When I picked it up to see why, long tendrils of melted satin dripped from the iron to the ironing board. Dad saw the dismay, even horror, on my face as he walked through the house at that very moment.

I expected a firm statement about being careful not to damage things. Instead, I watched as one of his impish grins spread over his dear face. Silently he made a graceful downward motion with his hand, reminiscent of the fall of molten fabric. His understanding, couched in humor, saved the day. In fact, that graceful motion of his hand became a secret joke we shared for weeks!

As a father, it's crucial for you to have rules and consequences and to follow up in enforcing them. It is even more important to be sensitive and to individualize. You must give your children credit for figuring out some things for themselves. If you spend time around them, you will discover what they know, and your job can be easier. I knew my mistake all too well. My face pictured the horror that became my best teacher. I rarely failed to accurately set that iron's temperature after that!

Dad taught us well to play. He knew we needed a social life that extended outside of our own family. Our home became the scene of countless parties. During the summer we staged watermelon feeds for the entire group of young people from our church and our neighborhood. A huge tank, full of icy cold water, stood near the big barn. After wonderful games, we all ate as much watermelon as we could hold. Few used the plates and utensils provided. Most grabbed immense slices and ate them right off the rind. Juice and seeds dripped everywhere. And it was OK. Outside there was no cleanup. It was pure joy!

In the winter there were occasional sledding parties. The 88-acre wheat field would be safe under a thick coating of ice. The cars, tractors, and even horses that pulled sleds did not dent the ice. Our town friends were overwhelmed by the immensity of the space, the ice, and the fun we created!

Partnering (remember that concept?) allowed our mother to make huge pots of hot chocolate, pumpkin pies, and other treats. Dad was the one who drove the horse and the treasured old family sleigh. He returned to the house an icicle but so pleased that once again he had provided the wholesome fun he knew we needed.

Let's summarize the principles these stories portray for you as a dad.

1. Find within you (or create it!) the spirit of playfulness it takes to be merry with your family.
2. Search for methods you can use to play with the children as well as your partner. Observe other dads, read, even rarely watch TV for good ideas.
3. Remember: play blends with work. Whenever possible, work together on major projects as a family. Collect good jokes to weave into conversation as you work together. Take time out once in a while during long jobs for a little treat and a review of accomplishments.

4. Make yourself play games your kids love. You may think you won't be able to endure it. Let me assure you: with the right spirit, not only will you endure it, but you'll learn to love it. Furthermore, you will find your children adoring you. How would they ever want bad friends or a gang membership when they have you?

5. I suspect Jesus had great fun fishing and walking on the water, at least during one stormy time. Try to think about how He would plan fun times with your family if He lived with you. He does, you know!

Just recall that "a merry heart doeth good like a medicine" (Prov. 17:22). You have God's age-old permission to laugh and have fun. You know, as well, that several studies have shown that laughter is therapeutic even in illnesses as serious as cancer. So take it if you can—the permission and challenge to lighten up and to laugh and play with your family. It will balance the heavy times and create strong bonds among you.

## Reflection and Action

1. List three of your favorite childhood games. Ask your spouse to do the same. Make plans to play one of these with your children in the upcoming days.

_____    _____

_____    _____

_____    _____

2. List three or four major projects that need to be done around

your house. Develop a plan for doing them as a family, including even the youngest members in the small responsibilities.

_____     _____

_____     _____

_____     _____

_____     _____

3. Ask your children to name their favorite games. Schedule a time to play one of these with your children in upcoming days.

_____     _____

_____     _____

_____     _____

4. Convene a family meeting and brainstorm inexpensive activities your family can do together (e.g., picnic, fish, play kickball, etc.).

_____     _____

_____     _____

_____     _____

_____     _____

# 5

# Father— a Disciplinarian

In chapter 2 we discussed Dad as a teacher about all sorts of wonders and discoveries. Now, even at the risk of overlapping, let's think about another sort of teaching and learning for which dads are needed.

This category of functioning is that of discipline. The word, of Latin derivation, means to teach and to learn. A disciple is a follower or an adherent of a great teacher or mentor. Discipline does *not* mean punishing. It may include some painful consequences to a child's wrong behavior or poor judgment; but more appropriately, it is the most effective process by means of which a child can learn how to live right. A good father disciplines his child by his example, by his establishment of rules or boundaries, and by his consistent follow-through in enforcing the rules. As we will use the word in this chapter, discipline refers to teaching right from wrong and requiring obedience, respect, and responsibility.

For four specific reasons, I've learned that a great many men are unwilling or afraid to accept this assignment of being a disciplinarian.

1. Many fathers grew up without a dad. They have no pattern to guide them. These men are deeply yearning for a father, and sometimes they unconsciously parent themselves through their children. Their dads let them get by with many misbehaviors because they were absent and didn't know the problems. Or on their "Disneyland Dad" weekends, they couldn't bear to spoil the fun by correcting their kids.

2. Boys who grew up without a dad had discipline from their moms if they received any at all. When they became fathers, they expected their wives to do all the correcting. It was far more comfortable for her to do it, since she was with the children most of the time anyway. So many moms deeply resent the failure of their husbands to help correct the kids. They fail to understand the lack of an example their husbands grew up with and struggle over.

3. Their dads were abusive to them. For some reason, many dads act as if the only way in the world to correct their children is to yell at them or spank them now and then. The spanking can so quickly turn into abuse, leaving deep wounds that slowly heal, with scars that last a lifetime. Later in this chapter we'll list some concise guidelines to help you.

4. Their wives do not understand their predicament. When men fail to correct the children properly (meaning: as the wives would do it!) or not at all, the wives criticize and even demean them. Few fathers can cope with such treatment, and they withdraw from the entire family into work, hobbies, or total isolation.

Let me share with you a few of my father's world-class disciplinary techniques. Starting with early childhood, I will try to help you find some guidelines to adapt for yourself.

## Early Childhood

I was a very young child, still sleeping in a crib. The weather was cool, and I was snuggled warmly under the lovely handmade quilts. Our farm had no electricity, so we lived with the soft glow of kerosene lamps. My lamp was lit, and my oldest sister was trying to sing me to sleep. Her soft voice and gentle manner soothed me, but not to sleep. Oh, no! I was loving every minute of this scene and the total focus of attention I was given.

Every so often this patient sister would tiptoe out of the room. Immediately I would cry, so she would graciously return and repeat the scene. I was loving it. She was not! After what seemed an eternity to her, she called downstairs to Dad. I can recall her frustrated words: "Daddy, I can't make her go to sleep, and I have to study. What shall I do?"

Dad's next words were very clear: "Gracie, if you don't cut out that crying, I'm coming up to spank you!" Now you must understand. I loved my dad. I did not comprehend "spank," and I was having too wonderful a time to stop abruptly. In fact, I thought maybe Dad would only add to the party. So I kept right on with my routine.

Perhaps one more verse of my song was all I got to cry before I heard a heavy tread on the old wood stairs—not a party-going tread! Only a minute later I knew a number of things I had not known before. None of them have I forgotten.

1. Most importantly, I knew Dad would always keep his word. For better or for worse, he would do exactly what he said.

2. I learned what a spanking was. While I do not now condone spanking, I knew that one, while not wonderful, was not too bad either. I had no afterpain, and I suspect I sustained no bruises. Dad had excellent self-control, which is often lacking in

today's fathers. At any rate, the consequence was worse than playing my game of Selfish.

3. I learned other people had rights and needs as much as I had a wish for attention and fun. I had to give up some of my wishes in favor of my sister's having time to study.

What a great many lessons for a little child to master in one evening! The event did not dent my love for my father or his for me. In fact, it increased my respect immensely. Never again did he spank me, but I didn't challenge him very badly either!

## Early Elementary School

Throughout the joy-filled years of childhood, I learned to read faces—especially eyes. The words of Ps. 32:8 are living words: "I will instruct thee and teach thee in the way which thou shalt go: I will guide thee with mine eye." Most of Dad's discipline of me came from his compassionate brown eyes. A serious look meant that I had pushed my boundaries as far as I ought to. A quick flash of anger said, "Do it! Now!" But a tiny twinkle told me I could afford a delay or one more word of defense.

Since I had learned that Dad wanted only and always what was best for me, I could see no reason to rebel. Getting my own way would have been fun indeed. But I had a great deal of fun with my sisters and friends. Keeping an open, loving bond with my dad was worth infinitely more to me than having my way.

Dads, your kids must know you love them if your long-term discipline can be used well and internalized. In order to work, love must be tough and protective at times as well as gentle.

## Preadolescence

The ages from 5 to 13 are years of a new sort of growth and learning. Social skills are a necessity as well as academic skills and some prowess in sports. These things are essential to self-esteem building and learning to get along in the big world.

For nearly 20 years, as a psychiatrist, I spent at least one day a week trying to help underachieving students, their teachers, and their parents. Part of my evaluation came to be the assessment of the responsibilities these young people carried at home. It was no surprise to me to discover that bright kids who did poorly in school were also capable kids who did almost nothing at home. Most parents asked their children to clean their rooms, empty the trash, or help with dishes. But all too few followed through to see to it their children completed their tasks.

By doing so, they deprived their children of some sense of achievement. These kids failed to develop a sense of responsibility. They built habits of carelessness and indifference that carried over into the other compartments of their lives. These days, many kids eventually quit school when it seems boring. They feel that all of life should be fun and easy.

Dads, you can help immensely to prevent such horrifying defeats. One middle school student told me this story. His father had just moved out of the home Dan shared with his mom. She had been unable to get his somewhat bulky body out of the house for several days to attend school. I actually made a house call to see what we could do to help this smart boy. Dan was polite to me, but he refused to budge out of the chair adjacent to his desk.

Finally his defenses wore down. Tears welled into his eyes and dripped onto his neat blue jeans. "I know what I need!" he blurted out. "I need my dad to come home and kick my rear. I just can't make it without him!"

Dan's sobs and tragic words could be repeated in hundreds of thousands of variations. An average of 25 percent of young people who enter high school never finish— so many of them because they have no dads to care enough to cheer them on and make them do what they have too little self-discipline to finish.

Perhaps you were one of those abandoned kids. You, too, needed a dad to symbolically "kick your rear" just a bit to keep you moving. How can you teach what your dad failed to teach you?

Here is one example of creative fathering for preteens. You may translate it into a modern setting. The truth is the same.

We cooked all of our food on a beautiful blue-enameled wood-burning cookstove when I was little. It became my task to gather kindling and fill the box that held sticks of wood for heat with which to cook breakfast. It was not too difficult, really. The huge stack of wood was carefully split and mounded not too far from the back door. All it took was three or four armfuls to provide enough fuel. But I found several clever ways to avoid the job I disliked intensely. The wood was heavy. It was edged in splinters. But mainly, I just loved to play or read. So, conveniently I forgot.

How often I had forgotten, I can't recall. But I vividly remember how I learned to stop forgetting. Here's what my father did.

Late one autumn evening, about 10:30 or later, I was sound asleep. A definitely unhappy masculine voice called me awake. It must have reminded me of my crib experience, because I hurriedly pounded down the 11 steps to the living room. I was in my warm flannel pajamas, my eyes were blurry from sleep, and my thoughts not too well focused either.

In Dad's characteristic fashion, he said no words. But once again, he taught volumes. His rough hand lay heavy on my shoulder as he guided me to the kitchen, the blue-enameled range, and the empty woodbox behind it. He pointed to the door, and I knew what I had to do. I stumbled through the door and down the path to the woodpile.

When I returned with a heavy load of scratchy hedge-wood, I realized Dad had watched over me because he held open the screen door so I wouldn't drop a stick.

Dad was fair. When there was enough wood to cook breakfast, he told me I could finish filling the woodbox in the morning. I recall a very important decision I made that evening: "I will never forget to fill this woodbox again."

Once again, consider all the points Dad taught through this disciplinary action.

1. I had important responsibilities. The entire family would miss a good hot breakfast without fuel for the stove.

2. Everyone else had his or her own jobs. No one else would rescue me from mine.

3. My father cared about me enough to inconvenience himself in order to teach me. It would have been easier by far for him to bring in the wood. He cared enough to take the harder route, to provide discipline, not permissiveness.

4. Even in the midst of his tough love, Dad was watching over me, protecting me, and willing to help me. Perhaps with one of my more strong-willed siblings, he would have used a different method; but Dad knew each of us and disciplined us accordingly. I trust he recognized my sensitive spirit and basically conscientious heart. His bit of grace for me once again motivated me much more than a really harsh consequence ever could.

## Teen Years

On Pearl Harbor Day, December 7, 1941, the United States finally declared war. What had been a base of support for the Allied forces in Europe became our war too. Overnight we knew my brother would be drafted. Our gasoline, tires, food, coffee, and just about everything we purchased became rigidly rationed. I was just a sophomore in high school, my older sister a senior. There would not be enough fuel for both the farm equipment and daily drives to and from school, some 17 miles a day.

There was no option for quitting school. Dad knew the absolute need for "as much education as you can possibly get." I suspect his and Mom's decision was one of the most difficult of their lives. My sister and I would live away from home in our own apartment in order to complete high school.

Our small town was the hub of the old Santa Fe Railroad. Any eastbound or westbound engine that needed to go north or south was placed on a huge roundabout that turned it to the track it needed to follow. The use of trains in the war years was mainly for troop and equipment transportation. You can see that meant our town of only 12,000 people was crowded with uniformed, glamorous (to all of the teenage girls), armed forces guys. Most of them were appallingly young, usually scared to death, but with their fear masked by a gallant swagger. Most of the girls were madly in love with their concept of heroism and were easy prey to ill-advised romantic involvement.

It was into this environment the two of us naive country girls moved. We were carefully placed in an upstairs studio apartment near our church. We never missed school or church events. We kept our apartment clean and cooked really good meals. We stayed out of countless troubles and grew up overnight. My older sister deserves much of the credit for our responsible independence. She was the one who made me help keep order.

But the truth is that neither of us would have disgraced our father or mother. Both of us were well aware of the prayers of Dad's partner, our mother, and so we made it.

When dads have trained their babies, taught them to love and laugh as children, and drilled into them a core of responsibility, then the children can be safely released to even an early era of separation if that should become necessary, as it was for us.

## How to Do It

Dads, I hope you can see how vitally important is your role as the disciplinarian of your children. Add to this the need for teamwork with your wife. As partners, your sense of balance and the evidence of parental strength will make you unbeatable in enforcing family rules and setting family boundaries.

Here is a list of specific steps to become a blue-ribbon teacher of life skills.

1. *Believe you can do it.* A father who doubts himself is not likely to enjoy much trust from his child. You have an unbeatable promise: "Yet from this same God you have received your standing in Jesus Christ, and he has become for us the true wisdom, a matter, in practice, of being made righteous and holy, in fact, of being redeemed" (1 Cor. 1:30, PHILLIPS). All you need to do is ask for God's wisdom and abide by His plan and promises.

2. *Use your partner.* In chapter 1, we learned how both of you as parents must discuss your goals for your children. How do you want them to not only behave but also *be* in that core of their lives? Together, how can you guide them to become that sort of being? Avoid power struggles in this process, but discuss all the information you can gather. Remember your childhood, and emulate those methods that helped you. Cancel out any disciplines that caused you to even *feel* like rebelling. And by all means, try to come up with some creative plans of your own. Partner with another father or a couple whom you believe to be good parents. Exchanging problems and successes

and brainstorming over new ideas can be fun and most helpful.

3. *Formulate a set of basic guidelines* or policies. These should be broad based and understandable by your children. Be careful to modify them according to your child's age and capabilities. Be sure you and your partner agree on these guidelines. Be clear about how they fit your goals for your child.

4. *Make a list of meaningful consequences* if the rules are broken. A stern word and look may be all some children require. Others may need you to put your arm around them and propel them to their task as my father did. Only extremely rarely may a child require a swat—and then only if you practice superb self-control. To be hit by an intensely angry father is more likely to create rebellion than obedience. Examples of consequences include: time-out, losing privileges, being assigned extra jobs, fixing something he or she broke, making an apology.

5. *Practice following through on consequences.* If you are too angry or too passive, either extreme will defeat your best results. You need to take all breaking of rules seriously. Your focus must stay on helping your child learn his or her lesson with the least severe consequences it will take to teach it. Being too severe creates rebellion or silent withdrawal. Too laid-back an attitude allows your child to believe he or she can get by with it and even do it again.

6. *Be generous with praise* when your child yields his desires to your fatherly commands. Even when a child obeys with a bad attitude, express your appreciation for the effort. The attitude will change if you are consistent over a length of time.

Discipline is a function that is dreaded by most fathers. I rather suspect my father anticipated it because he had become so good at it. Granted, he had a lot of experience with seven of us. I hope his successful ideas inspire you to develop your own adaptations. Above all, remember to stay in touch with God. His guidance and wisdom, already quoted, are yours instantly for the using.

## Reflection and Action

1. Recall a time from your childhood when you were disciplined hurtfully. Record your feelings about that time here. _____

_____

_____

_____

_____

2. Write a short paragraph about the difference between *punishment* and *discipline*. _____

_____

_____

3. Ask your spouse to write a paragraph about the way she was disciplined as a child. Discuss the differences in your upbringing and how they affect the ways you handle your children today.

_____

_____

_____

_____

4. Convene a family meeting to discuss the discipline policies in your home. Together, make a list of expectations, and outline the consequences for infractions. Post the list in a prominent place, and commit together to follow through with agreed-upon consequences.

_____        _____

_____        _____

_____        _____

_____        _____

_____        _____

_____        _____

5. Write each of your children's names below. List five things you respect or admire about them. Praise your children about those things this week.

_____        _____

_____

_____        _____

_____

_____        _____

_____

_____        _____

_____

# 6

## *Father—Values Sorter*

It is extremely disappointing to me that the second leading cause of death among teenagers in America is suicide. The years of life that should be filled with the joy of discovery and the excitement of adventure and planning for independence are times that are dark with despair. So many kids are without any meaning about life or purpose for life. Many of these young people are those whose fathers, in one degree or another, are missing from their lives.

While mothers tend to live out their values quietly, good fathers talk about them. A father's authority seems to be stronger than a mother's. Perhaps it's voice quality that makes the difference. Maybe children get used to moms, with whom they tend to spend most of their time. It could be that God made this difference so dads could, once again, be a bit of a model to children of God the Father. At any rate, Dad, take the role of the establishment of values seriously. Where you place each in your thinking and living will be keenly observed by your youngsters. They will follow your example rather than hearing only your words.

My local metropolitan newspaper invited me and a number of other people who worked with families and youth to meet and formulate a top 12 list of values. They purposed to feature one value each month in the proper section of the paper, explaining its significance and encouraging our entire community to both practice and teach these concepts—especially in the home. The group was as diverse as it could possibly be. We had Protestants, Catholics, Jews, Muslims, and agnostics. What a stimulating experience it was!

Here are the 12 top values sifted down from many that we finally listed:

1. Respect for self, others, and our world
2. Compassion
3. A sense of awe, wonder, trust, and faith
4. Tolerance
5. Integrity/honesty
6. Justice, fairness
7. Love of learning and reverence for wisdom
8. A sense of boundaries, limits, and propriety
9. Courage
10. Commitment, tenacity (not quitting)
11. Altruism, generosity, proper use of money
12. Understanding and commitment to right from wrong

This is an imposing list, yet each of us could add others. I'd like to have included a good sense of humor and the ability to play well. Also the ability to work hard, be conscientious, and be productive are important values to me. Undoubtedly you, too, have favorite philosophies for life that show great worth. We simply can't include all of them, so let's start with these 12 and think about how you can teach these priceless, timeless traits to your family.

## Respect

Most schoolteachers I know say their students have been growing increasingly disrespectful over the past 15 to 20 years. From kindergarten through high school, these reports are consistent. While some responsibility for this may rest with the schools themselves, I suspect most of it is from the loss of family values. Unfortunately, a huge number of families watch family-focused TV comedies regularly. The rudeness among these supposedly funny people is matched only by their cynicism. It is inevitable that some of the negative humor is mimicked by countless families.

So, fathers, if you want to be an instrument of change in your family, here's how.

1. Develop a core sense of self-respect. Act and speak in a manner that communicates to others that you are a good man. Walk and speak with strength. Stand erect. Think positively about yourself, your job, and your life.

2. Speak to and about your wife only with respect. In his classic research book, *The Antecedents of Self-esteem*, Dr. Stanley Coopersmith makes it clear that healthy, well-adjusted teenagers had parents who respected each other.[1] Learn to disagree and discuss controversial issues agreeably. Do not verbally abuse each other. Stick with the focus of any disagreement until you get it settled. Then return to harmony and respect of each other.

3. Learn to correct your children firmly and clearly before you get so upset with them you lose control of your emotions. The more you show respect for your child's mother in the process of discipline, the better. Few wounds hurt moms more than those inflicted by a husband who sides with the children against her. *Any disagreements involving children and their privileges must be settled away from them.* Otherwise they will soon learn which of you they can manipulate in order to get their way.

4. Make a ground rule that no one is to hurt anyone in your family in any way. You can discuss, disagree, and problem solve, but there is no reason to hurt one another. If one of you breaks that rule, there must be a consequence. Some families re-

quire a 25-cent fine. Others assess time-out, extra work, or the loss of a privilege. Find the one thing that is most meaningful to your child so he or she can best learn the needed lesson. And be sure to follow this rule carefully as parents also.

5. Remember to give lots of pats and words of affirmation for both efforts and successes. A child who struggles heroically to bend his or her will to yours deserves more respect, in a way, than does a child who finds it easy to give in.

6. Show respect for others—even when you may disagree with them. Jesus showed respect to everyone except the self-righteous people like the Pharisees. He treated sinners with special wisdom and acceptance. He's the best role model.

Respect comes from a Latin word meaning "to look at or to look back upon." What we see on the surface is not all there is to a person. It's what is inside that counts. Jesus had the capacity to see inside people. He knew whether they were honest in seeking truth or were only trying to prove that their way was the only correct one. We all would do well to follow in His steps.

## Compassion

In most of the examples of my father, I hope you can feel his compassion. Ps. 103:13 says it best: "As a father has compassion for his children, so the LORD tenderly sympathizes with those who revere Him" (MLB). You will recall that my father's tender sympathy for me never allowed him to rescue me or be very easy on me. What it so masterfully did was influence the *manner* in which he disciplined me. "Gentleness is always strong, and true strength is always gentle," said an old motto that I like to quote. That's what's great about good fathers.

Compassion means to feel with another. As a dad, remember how you felt as a boy. When you had goofed and you knew a really big consequence was pending, did you tremble inside? Were you afraid of your consequences? A little fear, perhaps, breeds respect. But excessive fear creates pain that causes rebellion later on. Sooner or later a child becomes an adolescent. When your child physically outgrows you, fear of your intensity will no longer work. Instead, rebellion and deception will wreak havoc. Prevent that by showing compassion.

In the six steps above (under Respect), substitute "compassion" for "respect," and you will know how to show it. Just add a seventh step: "Remember how you felt in circumstances similar to your child's." Try to give him or her what you needed and wanted at such a time.

## Sense of Awe and Wonder

The experiences Dad and I shared with the hatching chick, newborn farm animals, and sprouting seeds in the garden even now give me a sense of awe. A skyful of stars, a thunderstorm with the flashing lightning, roaring thunder, and strong winds humble me with their majesty. So does a singing mountain brook and the rasping noise of cicadas and crickets.

When my grandson was only four, he and I took a brief walk to a small park near his house. It grew dusk as we sat and listened to God's creation. I named for him all the noises of nature: croaking frogs, singing insects, wind through the trees, the good-night calls of the birds were only some of the awe-filled sounds. Andy crept slowly onto my lap, and we shared intimately the wonders of sound and sight. You don't have to live on a farm to teach the wonder of squirrels leaping and birds flying. You only need to be aware and willing to take time to share the wonder.

How long has it been since you took time to focus on God's creation? Have you ever taken time to teach your child about His wonders?

Within only a few miles of most places in America there are layers of rocks shoved out to make room for roads. Within those dry rocks are more wonders that will surprise you. You are likely to discover fossils from ages past. You may happen to find a geode with sparkling crystals inside. You may find amazing shell creatures even in the heart of America. This very summer, some of my family members found immense freshwater clams (at least eight inches across) on the dry shore of a large lake.

Just take the time to explore, and you will discover. Open your mind to learn and your heart to revel in the amazing creativity of the Heavenly Father. I hope He will challenge you to new heights of creativity in fathering!

## Tolerance

Where I grew up, there were few people who were different from us. There were some people from Germany who still spoke their native language, but they worked and worshiped about as we did. There were some Amish folks with their unique garb and vehicles. But they exchanged work with us and ate at our table during harvest season. There were a few lovely olive-skinned, dark-eyed Hispanics whose dads worked for the railroad. We were comfortable with most of them.

Not quite as comfortable for me was attending the high-steepled large Catholic church in our town once for Christmas Eve mass. For me it was awesome nearly to the point of fear. Their worship style was tremendously different from what I was used to, yet I saw every member of that vast audience solemnly celebrate the birth of the same Jesus I knew. They reverently accepted Communion, believing the elements were the very body and blood of Christ given for their sins. Later, when I talked about my impressions, I felt incredible relief when my father said, "If every Catholic loves Christ and trusts and follows Him the best they know how, they will make it to heaven." Those words from my father watered the seeds of tolerance in my heart.

Nearly every August, we expected a dinner guest. We never knew when he would drive in, but we all recognized his old truck. We knew it would be loaded with wonderfully juicy apples. From her secret sugar bowl, Mom would find the money it took to buy some. Tactfully the little man would give us kids a free sample, and inevitably he was invited to join us for a noontime dinner. He knew what a good cook our mom was, so he planned his arrival time carefully. Dad was most friendly to him and enjoyed discussing all sorts of topics with him.

One day our apple peddler looked skeptically at the delicious roast Mom served. With embarrassment he asked, "Missus, is this pork?" When she replied that indeed it was, he politely refused a serving.

I waited until he left before I asked my father why the man wouldn't eat pork. With kindness Dad explained how Jews obeyed God's laws in the Old Testament, which were carefully written to protect them. I silently admired our guest's courage and knew we loved him and could share our food and faith with him. The attitude of my parents was a huge step in learning and practicing tolerance.

## Integrity/Honesty

In today's world, from children to corporations, the idea exists that anything you want to do is OK, as long as no one knows. In many families, dads tell the children to report to callers that he's not there. But kids know he is there. In those families, little white lies and big black ones are condoned. Stealing items from the workplace has become a multimillion-dollar problem.

Healthy families do not buy into such practices, and wise fathers will neither allow it nor practice it. The example of my father's willingness to pay back $5 he believed he did not owe is quite a demonstration of integrity. It requires knowing and accepting oneself unconditionally to evidence integrity. What I believe and how I live must be precise carbon copies.

Today's Christian world is embarrassingly full of well-known people who do not show integrity. They loudly proclaim one set of values while secretly living by quite another.

To be an example of an honest father with integrity requires several fundamental practices.

1. You must be clear about your beliefs in all areas of life.
2. You must practice those beliefs all the time—not just when you think someone is watching. For example, you must never lie, cheat, or steal. You must show respect for others, live responsibly, and pay your debts—yes, even credit cards!
3. Talk about your values with your family, and let each one know what you expect from him or her. Praise each one who evidences an attempt to live up to your teaching of honesty. But don't discuss any values until your life backs up its teaching.

Integrity means that you weave into your very character all the strands of your life experiences. Godly fathers do not practice the denial of truth. If you've made a mistake, you own up to it, correct it, and avoid repeating it. If it's appropriate, ask forgiveness, even from your children. If you have suffered a loss, you may grieve, but don't whine and fall into self-pity. Pick up the tag ends of your tapestry, knot them, and move on with the weaving.

You can teach your children how to live well if you understand and practice profound honesty and integrity.

## Justice and Fairness

One of the more common complaints of kids is "That's not fair!" Usually by this they mean that they've been given the short end of the stick. Their siblings have easier tasks, less severe punishments, or more desirable privileges. Usually the perceived injustices are a child's view of things. The sibling was corrected privately, so the complaining child did not know its severity. The privileges were earned in a way the child did not understand.

The point is that all of us seek fairness from early childhood on. Justice, in the legal sense, is widely believed to be nonexistent these days. A wife of some 40 years, abandoned by her husband, recently received not one penny of support from her spouse due to a calloused judge. In a similar case, a wife not only did not get support but also had to pay a substantial amount of child support from a meager salary to her well-to-do professional husband. We are all well acquainted with the media portrayal of "justice."

We can sit around and complain, or we can begin at home to create a sense of fairness and real justice. Let me give you an example.

Justin, 10, and Katie, 12, were arguing intensely about who should get to use the computer. When Dad had heard enough of their disagreement, he called both children to him. He handed each of them a pad of paper and a pencil with these instructions: "I want each of you to pretend you're an attorney. Write out your case. List all the reasons why you should have the next turn at the computer. Then come and present it to me. I'll be the judge."

The assignment took a long time, but the children took it seriously. With logic and a search for fairness, the children's approach was transformed from fighting to fairness. Dad, the judge, was able to formulate a way in which each child could use the computer. Perhaps if every father could help his children understand and practice justice at home, our world could once again return to healthy justice.

## Love of Learning and Reverence for Wisdom

"It's time for your homework now, Derek," called his father.

"But I don't have any homework, Dad," said Derek.

This response puzzled Dad because he'd studied every night of his more than 16 years of schooling. So he checked with his son's teacher, who verified that she rarely assigned homework. Dad and his wife (partner) discussed the issue. It was appealing to think they would not have to be the bad guys who made their son work every evening. On the other hand, there was so much for every child to learn with so many decades of exponential information growth, no child could learn it all in school. Furthermore, they were aware that Derek's primary goal in life was becoming only pleasure. They knew life had to have a bigger focus than fun.

Dad found a time when Derek was available and looked as if he might be willing to think with him. The father explained his observations and concerns. He asked Derek about a compromise. If he were allowed ample playtime and a little TV time, would he be willing to commit some time to studying? Reluctantly, Derek, a fifth grader, agreed that he would. He proposed 15 minutes, but Dad held firmly to at least half an hour. Before tests, the time might increase to a full hour.

Somewhat angrily, Derek followed through. Dad knew it would be difficult, so he arranged some paperwork of his own nearby. Occasionally he would stop and quiz Derek over spelling words or discuss the meaning of a book the boy had to report on. Before either one realized it, Derek began to see that it was fun to get perfect papers and to really comprehend the content of books. He was prepared for each school day and confident in class.

Dad and Mom both found intellectual growth with Derek. They began to talk over dinner about ideas they had and events they had thought about with positive and critical minds during the day. It was not only Derek but also the entire family who began to love learning.

When you consider expanding learning to spiritual,

emotional, and all parts of life, you can see why this value was in our group's top 12. I hope you'll include it in yours.

*Cruden's Concordance*, a classic reference for every word in the Bible, has four and a half columns of verses about wisdom. The Bible is, in fact, a collection of the wisdom of God over the ages of time.

Wisdom is defined as "the power of judging rightly and following the soundest course of action based on knowledge, experience, understanding, good judgment, discretion, and sagacity."[2]

It seems to me wisdom is the capacity to apply knowledge to all of life's perplexities. Many of them will be understood through this use of wisdom, and the rest can be accepted for now, to be resolved later as wisdom grows.

Some youngsters seem wise early on in their lives. Others achieve wisdom in the teen years with physiological growth of their neurological system. (Most parents of teens will not believe this!) And some people never seem to acquire the ability to be wise.

It was my father who taught me wisdom. He could apply to almost any event the acknowledgment of God's hand. Though I never knew Dad to miss church, I will equally recall his statement that by walking through a wheat field he heard a sermon as clearly as from the pulpit. I, too, began to recognize sermons in rainbows and storms, in crickets and cardinals.

You may recall my father's teaching me about the hatching of baby chicks. From that day, I thought of babies only as the products of God's miraculous creation.

One cold January day, my brother was attending to the birth of a lamb. The mother ewe was struggling, and he was totally focused on the two animals. At last the lamb was safely delivered. My brother only then looked up and discovered that his 10-year-old daughter had silently scrutinized the entire scene. He grinned at her as she commented, "Oh, Daddy! It's exactly as you told me!" She had previously asked her father to tell her about the birth of babies. He had described the wonder of it all as best and simply as he could. His honesty had paid off, but his wisdom had given her a sense of reverence and awe for both life and wisdom.

The power of a father's words, remember, is irreplaceably great. Never leave the teaching of your children to their mother alone. Her wisdom, too, is a matchless gift to children. But this book is dedicated to you as a father. Practice applying your gift of wisdom, and pass it on to your children!

## Sense of Boundaries and Propriety

It's easy for me to understand the many children who hate doing dishes! I was one of them. When I was growing up, there were usually at least 10 of us for every meal, and often there were guests. Furthermore, since we had neither electricity nor running water, we had to heat the water on the stove and rinse the dishes through scalding water from a huge kettle. They had to be dried and put away. If we missed some dried food, the piece had to be washed over again.

One summer day, I developed a headache right after lunch. Without doubt I dramatized it somewhat, but Dad said I could go and lie down until I recovered. By that time, my long-suffering sisters had completed the dish washing. What a deal I had discovered! Get sick after meals, and you get out of dish washing!

The very next day I tried it again. Here's what happened. Dad had been taught with remarkable scientific accuracy that the tongue was an accurate diagnostic tool. If it was unusually red, very likely one had a fever. A tongue with whitish coating indicated an upset stomach, and so on. On this day, Dad asked me to stick out my tongue. I knew my game was up, but Dad's wisdom put the physical evidence in focus instead of an angry power struggle. I knew my tongue was OK, and so did he. So off to the kitchen sink I trudged. Dad had set the boundary well for honesty and manipulation. When I was really sick, I went to bed. When I was truly well, I carried my responsibilities.

Few people I know love to read as much as I do. As a child I read and reread every book, magazine, or available printed material voraciously. My father, too, was an avid reader, but he knew when to put a book down. I didn't. My chores and even playtime went unnoticed as I buried myself in my reading.

Disciplining wisely and meaningfully was one of Dad's strengths. One day Dad asked me to sit down for a talk. There was no twinkle in his eye as he told me I would not be doing any reading for a week. I recall asking in astonishment, "Not even the funnies, Dad?" With only a bit of hesitation, he replied, "Not even the funnies."

I could tell this boundary made Dad almost as sad as it did me. He loved to read, so he understood my love. But he knew I had no boundaries between reading, responsibilities, and the need of physical play.

That week was one of the longest in my life. But at the end the lesson was mastered. I could read—only when I had done my jobs, played with my sisters, and lived a bit of real life.

Your child may need social boundaries, sleep time boundaries, limits on TV times and programs, computer use boundaries, or some limits on language and interpersonal action. Your job description, fathers, must include respect for boundaries.

In the 1960s Dr. Stanley Coopersmith did a landmark study of well-adjusted, healthy teenagers. Among other things, he discovered that a foundational element in their lives was the presence of clearly defined boundaries in these families. Each family studied had slightly varying limits, but all of them knew where the limits were, and they could flex only a little bit.[3]

Once limits were established, each child knew it was a waste to test them out. They were fixed. Settling within the boundaries, then, enabled the children to play and work with all of their energy. They found fun and successes by focusing on what they *could* do. They didn't need to waste their energy on finding out what they could *not* do.

So, as a dad, work to build fences that will stand. Expand them as your children grow, but keep the children aware that there are always some limits in life. Hopefully, the fence posts that hold those boundaries will be those values you will demonstrate and pass on to them.

## Courage

Most thoughtful people feel concerned about the secularism, even atheism, that has subtly invaded our Christian community. One by one and under various disguises we are losing many of our freedoms. It is very tempting to align oneself with the popular cause or person. I have more than once faced the challenge of being the only one in a group to speak up for a cause that God and I, alone, seemed to believe in. Never have I regretted speaking for truth as I see it or as God's Word portrays it. But it is not easy.

Having the courage to risk helping another in danger is worthy of cheers even from our jaded media. Upon occasion I watch the TV series *911*. Scene after scene somehow is found from real life depicting many heroic people who willingly risk their lives to help someone in imminent danger.

How do fathers portray courage to their families? Here's another example of my father's greatness. It happened when I was in fourth grade and my older sister was in sixth. We awoke one bitterly cold January morning to find ice everywhere. The car wouldn't start, and even the ever faithful tractor made not a sound when Dad tried to start it.

We had to get to school. Staying at home or expecting school to close were not options! The risk of frostbite was the concern of our parents. We had to walk half a mile directly into the subzero north wind. Our parents bundled us into as many layers of warm clothing as they could get on us. Still I could tell they were worried.

At the last minute our dad decided to go with us. He had never done that, and I was so excited to have him along. He, too, bundled up warmly and walked ahead of us down the hard-frozen, rutted dirt road. As we went, Dad realized his body was not big enough to adequately protect his two girls. With no evident hesitancy, he opened his overcoat and held it out like ship sails. Each of us girls walked safely, protected by Dad's warm woolen coat.

What I learned later was Dad's belief that extreme cold could cause pneumonia. He had suffered pneumonia only a few years earlier and had nearly died from it. Yet he exposed himself to the relentless cold, risking recurrent illness and even possible death to protect us. His courage remains my model!

Jesus showed us the ultimate courage. To provide our salvation, He didn't just *risk* death. He *chose* death on a cross, so we would be well and whole in Him.

Once again, Dad, look for opportunities to show courage, to defend your families from the dangers of our era of time. Speak up, take appropriate action, and provide the shelter of your love and faith as you walk before your children.

### Commitment

This quality is another found in Nick Stinnett and John DeFrain's book *The Six Secrets of Strong Families*.

The more than 3,000 families he studied were firmly committed to each other as individuals and to the family as a unit. Such commitment seems to be lost in today's Western culture. Divorce is frequent and fairly easy. Abandoning children has become newsworthy and quite common.

People are ready to change jobs if it even seems advantageous. Some 25 percent of high school kids drop out, and in some areas, the percentage is much higher. The hedonistic philosophy, "What's in it for me?" seems to dominate people's thinking.

You must set the right example, fathers. Here's another role model.

When I was 14, a freshman in high school, our mother developed heart trouble and was confined totally to bed. There was no household help to be found in those early years of the war. We solemnly discussed which of the four girls should quit school and stay home with Mother. She recalled having to quit school in the seventh grade to stay with her mother.

Dad's face was solemn and his brown eyes a bit misty as he thought of a solution. He certainly didn't want to risk Mom's health. But he didn't want us to drop out of school. Finally he stated, "I'll do it! You girls can help on Saturdays and in the evenings. But I can cook, clean, and do the washing. No one quits school!" That settled it. And indeed he did all the necessary household tasks as well as keeping up the heavy farmwork. To my amazement he could bake bread nearly as good as Mom's. He did most of the laundry and just about every task imaginable.

Think of all the commitments his decision included. He certainly was committed to his partner and nursed her back to health. He stuck tenaciously to his profound belief in the value of education. He himself was committed to learning and performing new skills. He did them well, never thinking of them as "women's work," therefore beneath him. In fact, he acted excited about his new role of housefather.

Are you committed? Or do you come home, prop up your feet, and watch TV as you read the paper? Your wife has been working all day also. She and your children need a picture of you helping in the kitchen, giving baths, and running the vacuum.

## Generosity

During the grim years of the Great Depression, people throughout America endured unbelievable deprivation. Money was certainly scarce at our house. Clothes were scrounged from older siblings and generous relatives. New furniture or household items simply didn't exist for us. Occasionally new dishes came in big boxes of oatmeal. Flour sacks were fabric, as were salt and sugar containers. Such fabrics were bleached and made into patchwork sheets and underwear. So we survived quite well.

But we never lacked food. Our carefully tended hens laid eggs, the well-pastured cows gave wonderful foamy buckets of milk that were rich in cream. Uncles, aunts, and cousins arrived every autumn for huge butchering "fests" that provided good fresh meat for all of us. Our gardens fed us well and provided vegetables throughout the winter.

What the depression brought that still haunts my mind was a human stream of vagrants—hoboes, we called them. Men who could not support their families or even themselves left home and wandered about the country. They would hop on freight trains and go to other towns, hoping to find work or shelter.

Rumor has it that any hobo who found a place to get food or shelter in a barn or even a haystack would carve a sign on trees or fence posts so their buddies could also find help. Our farm must have had several such signs because we had a regular trail of visitors. My mother fed them fabulous meals and offered them water to drink and wash in. But she knew, as did they, that they were pestered by head lice, so they never entered our house.

They never minded, seemed grateful for the food, and sometimes offered to chop wood to pay for their meals. None of them ever stole from us, and I came to see them as a normal part of life.

People who lived in towns around us often came to visit for an evening or a Sunday. Few of them had the gardens and other great foods we had. I cannot remember any visitor leaving without some fresh garden vegetables and eggs. The generosity of my family left its mark upon me. I love being able to give to others, and I've learned that it's really only what we give in Jesus' name that we get to keep in the long run.

So teach your children to give to their church. And add to that some direct giving. I've not seen hoboes for years. But I've seen inner-city children with few or no toys, no coloring books, and no books to entice them to want to read. Perhaps you could encourage your children to sort through their clothes and toys once a season. They could give their outgrown but good items to children who have so little.

Holidays are a natural time to give to needy families. Imagine if every average family adopted one underprivileged family, gave food and gifts to them, and loved them—what a difference it would make in our deprived neighborhoods.

Generosity must be guided. We all know of groups and individuals who are con artists. They know how to grow rich on donations made to people and causes that see very little, if any, of the gifts. Be careful to check out the recipients of your giving, but don't let the charlatans make you bitter.

## Right over Wrong

I find many parents struggle—not over a *commitment* to right but with confusion over what *makes* anything right or wrong.

With all of my father's wisdom and the wonder of his

other qualities, I cannot recall that he ever taught me exactly what makes anything right or wrong. Generally I believed if he said so, that's the way it was. Period. Equally and much more, I believed if the Bible said so, that was it.

But the permission to think, to learn, and to grow—those values I learned. So I thought, learned, and grew. Throughout my late teen years and into my 20s I explored. Here are the gleanings from my mental calisthenics. As a father, you may have them. Check them out against your life experiences and God's Word. Adapt them to your thinking.

*Right*

1. Anything that matches biblical truth and commands is clearly right.
2. God's Word is for our good, so anything we do that is good for us is right. Promoting our physical, emotional, mental, and, above all, spiritual health is good for us. They are right.
3. Whatever we do should bring good upon those around us. Being thoughtful, kind, helpful, and generous makes our families secure and loving. These are right.
4. Doing right will usually open up new opportunities. Studying well may bring about educational and career opportunities. Working hard may prove reliability and earn advancements. (In today's politically oriented world, these results do not always happen!)
5. Something is right if it opens opportunities for, and brings good upon, people around us. If your child learns to team up with peers, helping them succeed as well as succeeding himself or herself, that is right.

*Wrong*

1. Practicing habits that constrict our lives and nar-

row our options are wrong. Choosing too much play over work (such as dropping out of school because it requires more than one wants to give) is wrong. Smoking, drinking alcohol, and abusing drugs are wrong because they endanger health and permit other damaging behaviors. Practicing promiscuous sex puts life and health in grave danger. It endangers the partner too.

2. Doing things that put others at risk of danger is also wrong. Gossiping or even telling truths that could hurt another's reputation are wrong. Inviting others to do things that are bad for them is wrong. Inviting an alcoholic to have a glass of wine is wrong. Most dads wouldn't do that, but lots of rebellious teens do exactly that. You must teach your teens why that is wrong.

3. Allowing one's mind to be open to destructive and erroneous thinking is wrong. Our minds are to be open to truth, so we do not dare to develop narrow, closed minds. But we need to protect our minds with the screens of God's Word and the Holy Spirit. Even God's own children can be deceived, so we must cautiously balance an open mind with these screens.

As a dad, you are the protector and teacher of your children. Look carefully for opportunities to set boundaries that are logical and fair for your families. These "Rights" and "Wrongs" weave together with the other 11 values mentioned previously to make one wonderful safety net!

## Balance

In all areas of our lives it is easy to get caught in extreme ends of a spectrum. Being too intellectual can rob us of emotions. Being just without practicing mercy creates intolerance. Becoming too tolerant can allow us to lose standards.

Walking circumspectly is a biblical injunction in both the Old and New Testaments. Exod. 23:13 orders God's people, "And in all things that I have said unto you be circumspect." In Eph. 5:15, Paul says, "See then that ye walk circumspectly, not as fools, but as wise."

Circumspection literally means "looking all around." We need not become paranoid, only cautious. So, fathers, consider this as one more value—circumspection. Practicing it will guide you in understanding your family's needs, setting up adequate protection, and enjoying each member.

There are few areas of weakness in Christian families as crucial as teaching values. Schools no longer try to do it. Even Sunday School and the church can do it only to a limited extent. It's difficult, but only you can do it. So learn to do it well. The Heavenly Father will help you anytime you ask if you listen and follow His guiding.

## Reflection and Action

1. Review the list of values Dr. Ketterman discusses early in this chapter. Identify the 5 that you consider most important.

_____

_____

_____

_____

_____

2. Think about the kind of humor used in your home. Is it hurtful to others, sarcastic, or rude? Write about a time that you were

made fun of. Ask your spouse and children to name something that hurts their feelings. _____

_____

_____

_____

_____

3. Dr. Ketterman says, "Compassion means to feel with another." Identify three areas that you think your children might be struggling with (e.g., a bad report card, a weight problem, a friend that moved away). Describe how you think they may be feeling about those struggles.

_____     _____

_____

_____     _____

_____

_____     _____

_____

4. Take the 5 values you identified in question 1, and write a sentence about why they are important to you. Share these sentences with your family. _____

_____

_____

_____

_____

_____

5. Review the 12 values Dr. Ketterman lists. Identify 3 that you can work to improve in your own life in the coming year. Ask your spouse and children to hold you accountable for improvement in these areas. _____

_____

_____

_____

# 7

# *Father— Believer in Me*

It could happen anytime to any one of the seven of us children. It always made a total impact on me. Dad would catch me off guard, look me square in the eyes, and ask firmly, "Grace, do you think you'll ever amount to anything?" Now you know from the stories about my father that he was never a mean person. But his tone of voice in asking this oft repeated question would grab my thoughts. I had to consider what he meant. What was it to "amount to something"? Did Dad doubt me?

My own answers thrust me like a jet stream into a challenging way of life. I discovered that amounting to something meant making a difference in my God-assigned arena of life. As a child I had no way to even imagine how small or large, easy or difficult that could be. The more I matured, the more certain I became that Dad never doubted me. He trusted me to live properly on my own at only 15 years of age. If there was doubt of my integrity from anyone else, my father never shared it. He believed in me.

Dad's questions motivated me to work hard and be a

person of strength, dignity, and integrity. But his unwavering belief in me taught me to believe in myself.

But it was not enough to just believe in myself either! If I ever did a sloppy job, Dad would show me how to do it right. Then he would watch me do it right until we both knew I could be proud of my work. Many years later, I wrote up a protocol for a juvenile judge with whom I worked. He praised me for the thoroughness of my work. Then he said, "You must be Pennsylvania Dutch!" That is exactly my heritage. Through his comments, I could hear Dad's voice echo, "*Now* you've done it right!" There's a right way and a wrong way. My dad valued right.

In order to communicate strength and poise to others, Dad believed we should walk erect and in our facial expression look at least pleasant, if not always confident. It was easy, especially in the hot summertime, to let one's body droop. Fatigue or disappointments could also create slumped shoulders and a sour face.

Whenever Dad saw this, he would give us a firm thump on the back and say in his stronger voice, "Grace, walk straight. Show some good pride. Don't act as if you're ashamed to be alive!" To this day I appreciate Dad's no-nonsense reminders. I believe that some of how we feel about ourselves contributes to the way we walk and how we look. I also know that when we make ourselves look good and walk straight, we feel better.

Gary Smalley's book *The Blessing* is a fascinating parallel between the father's legacy to his children in the Old Testament and today's father's gifts to his sons and daughters. His book is well worth reading, for he lists five ways in which fathers give a blessing (or fail to do so) to their children. I won't list them all, but Gary's beliefs align with my own.

A good father can give no greater gift to his child, I believe, than to find every good point in each child. He needs to describe it to the child, discussing how that gift can bless the child both now and in the future. Gary Smalley believes the father's blessing is the prediction of good for his children's future.

After a seminar I taught in a high school PTA, a mom and dad waited until I had time to talk with them. They had a 15-year-old son who was careless, sloppy, unmotivated, and an overall major disappointment to them. I had no doubts about either their love or concern for this son.

During our conversation, I asked what they had already tried to do to motivate this young man to change. The father began to list many dire predictions he had given to his boy: He would never amount to anything. (What a difference in his negative prediction and my father's thought-provoking question!) He would probably never do anything more than dig ditches. And there were more.

As I suggested the power of affirmation versus the destruction of negative, self-fulfilling "curses," the dad's face lit up. He'd never thought of the self-defeat he had set up for his son and the damage he'd unwittingly done to his son. He'd unconsciously believed the horrible predictions would motivate his son to want to be better. But the worst of the reverse was evident. The young man could see no hope of redemption. He was bad, so he would act badly. And he did. I dared to hope this scenario would change.

Remember, as a dad, your life and your words are powerful! Make them a power for the blessing of your children.

## Sons Need a Male Role Model

Many people recognize the truth in this book's introduction. Sons do better in life when they have a good, positive relationship with their father. Dads must believe in the masculinity of their sons. It's easy for many fathers to turn over their children's training and discipline to their mothers. And it is all too easy for a young son to identify with his mom, leaving sexual identity confusion to be dealt with later.

Your sons need to wear your boots and walk in your footsteps. They must learn your definition of maleness and feel your pride in their growth toward that. They also need your awareness that masculinity and femininity have variations. If your son is slightly built or not very physically coordinated, accept him as he is. He will probably not live through football or, perhaps, even soccer. But he may be a gifted teacher, artist, or musician. And that's OK. Unconditional love accepts each child as he is, encourages his gifts, accepts his weaknesses, and blesses him with predictions of a good future. When you gain your wisdom and love from God, you can offer this blessing!

## And So Do Daughters

It's easy for most people to understand why boys need a dad as a male role model. But many folks have not thought about the extreme importance of a male role model for girls.

For nearly 30 years I have worked with teenage pregnant girls. For several years we had in-depth psychological testing done to see if there were personal problems that had contributed to the complex issue of unplanned pregnancies. In some 80 percent of the cases, those young women had very poor relationships with their fathers. They described Dad as being gone a lot as in job requirements, asleep on the sofa, or glued to TV or a newspaper. One girl described showing her grade card to her father. It was an especially good report, and she yearned for her father to show his pride in her efforts. Instead, he threw it on the floor, never missing a frame of his TV show. It was not long after this event that she began having sex and soon became pregnant.

Repeatedly we found the young women sought older boyfriends. It is logical to suspect they were, unconsciously perhaps, seeking a man to fill the father vacuum they had experienced.

Please review the evidence of Dad's vital importance to their sons *and* daughters. It's in the introduction along with references to the studies that reveal the facts. If you already see the truth, then here are some guidelines for change—if you are one of the many dads who need to change.

1. Understand that it's not convenient or easy to be a parent. It takes time away from your personal interests and rest. Give that time gladly!

2. You cannot yield to the common belief that because you worked hard all day, the evening hours are yours. Chances are your wife also worked hard all day and needs a break. But most of all, your children have not seen you all day, and they desperately need to know you!

3. The best gift you can give your children is two parents who love and respect each other. Show them this by treating your spouse with warmth. Listen to her with respect, and help her with compassion. I urge all parents to sit down together briefly early each evening. They need to review the day and plan the evening in order to stay in touch and run the household right.

4. Each child needs a bit of individual time with his or her dad. And all the kids need time together with their dad. Whenever I visit my son-in-law, I know what I will see—he and three precious sons will be gardening, reading together, or playing soccer or some other sport. He has an uncanny knack of focusing in on each child while also making a team out of them.

5. My daughter recalls vividly that it was her father who taught her the skills she most loves now. He showed her how to ride her bike, roller-skate, snow-ski, and water-ski. He worked long hours filled with stress, yet he took time out of his own

need meeting to teach her. It was time well spent with high returns in a loving adult relationship. He also taught her how to choose that good father of her children.

6. Old habits are hard to break. If you really mean business, here are some tiny steps that will help.

   a. After work give yourself 5 to 10 minutes to sit quietly, review your day, and file it away, mentally, at work. Pray for strength and try to imagine precisely what Jesus would do with your family if He were in your place, after arriving home.

   b. When you get home, use your strongest willpower to stay away from your old habitual ritual. Substitute an action from your recent meditation with Christ.

   c. I suggest you first get into comfortable clothes and then give hugs and greetings all around. Let each child know you have a special time planned for him or her.

   d. Next, it's great to get your wife to spend those few minutes with you. Assign special jobs to the kids that make them work with each other in order to give you that private time together. It may well demand some training time so the children will not tear down the house in those minutes you are alone.

   This time together is for the mutual needs of both of you, not just one. I hope it includes affection, but mainly it's for thinking, planning, and sharing.

   e. Now it's time to follow your plan. One of you can finish dinner while the other plays with children or, better yet, enlists them in straightening the home. Even toddlers can help in this task.

   f. During dinner I urge you to promote family

communication. The TV or any distracting noises are out. Telephone calls can wait. Share an anecdote from your day, then try to elicit some event from each child as well as your wife. At first children may resist if this is not a familiar routine. Don't scold or force them. Just continue your own plan with your wife. They are almost certain to join in, in their own time. You can see this is another way to show each child your interest in him or her individually, blessing them, and uniting the family as well.

g. Finally, find out what each child needs to do during the evening. Schoolkids may have a project to do for tomorrow. It's so nice to discover it before the stores that sell poster board are closed!

h. While kids scatter off to their evening chores (be certain they have some), you and your wife can help each other with the jobs you have already planned.

i. Be sure to collect the family back together before bedtime. Occasionally watch TV together, more often play a game, or best of all, talk and listen to each other for a while.

j. I love the idea of tucking children in bed with big hugs and little prayers.

k. Finally, it's time for you and your partner. Try to take turns doing what each of you enjoys when the house or apartment gets still. Reading, listening to your music, just being near each other, or finding some time for romance are suggestions. It's so crucial that you partners stay close if you want to have a healthy family.

As you gradually see your family becoming a loving, supportive unit, you will see that your fatherly investment of both time and energy makes it all worthwhile.

# Reflection and Action

1. List three activities you enjoy doing. Name the last time you took the time to do one of those activities. If you aren't taking any time for yourself, schedule one of those activities in the next two weeks.

_____

_____

_____

2. Write a brief schedule of your after-work routine below. What are some ways you can improve your quality of life during these evening hours?_____

_____

_____

_____

_____

3. Write each of your children's names and two sentences about your hopes and dreams for their future. Consider sharing your thoughts with your children.

_____

_____

_____

_____

_____

_____

_____

_____

_____

4. Convene a family meeting. Pray a prayer of blessing over each one of your children, allowing God to lead your thoughts and words. _____

_____

_____

# Conclusion

The ability to become the father of the strong family you want lies in you as a man. Everywhere I go, I discover men who say, frankly, they really don't know how to do it. They had no role models—not even negative ones. How can they get from where they are to where they want to be?

I've already mentioned some ways. You have already read this book. Look for others. Go to places where families are—parks, museums, entertainment parks. Observe other dads. Choose from their interactions the activities that appeal to you. Adapt them to your own personality, and experiment with them. *Don't* lose your own personhood by trying to *be* someone else.

Try to recall your childhood and what you may have wished for from your father. Try giving those acts to your kids. But remember that your children are *not* you. So if they aren't excited about this idea, back off.

Perhaps the best source of information about successful fathering is your own children. Observe how they play and what each loves best. Ask if you may join in for a while. Ask them what they'd like you to do with them. Be prepared with a list of your own activities to offer.

Don't be put off. If at first the kids are reserved, it's probably that they feel shy. They may not know what to do if you are one of the "big new change" fathers. I suggest you set up the time and stick with it, but give them the choice of how you all spend it. They will learn along with you how wonderful being a sharing family can be.

Above all, take time to pray. Good prayer means listening as well as pleading. I often sit in a chair and try to imagine Jesus as He was on earth, sitting nearby. I ask specific questions and try to get my mind quiet. Always, God puts in my brain the most useful ideas, creative and new. My job, then, is to follow through and use them.

Remember, God loves your children, and He also loves you. You are a partner not only with your wife but also with the Heavenly Father. He has promised every resource you will ever need. Search His Word, practice conversational prayer, and use the practical common sense God gave every one of us. In Him you, too, can be a world-class father.

# Notes

**Introduction**

1. Kyle Pruett, "What's Behind the Fatherhood Debate?" *Report, Family Resource Coalition,* 15, No. 1 (Spring, 1996): 4-5.

2. James Levine and Edward W. Pitt, "Child Development: The Difference Dad Makes," ibid., 8-10.

3. Ross Parke, *Fathers* (Cambridge, Mass.: Harvard University Press, 1996).

4. John Snarey, *How Fathers Care for the Next Generation* (Cambridge, Mass.: Harvard University Press, 1994).

5. David Blankenhorn, *Fatherless America* (New York: Basic Books, 1995), 38.

6. David Popenoe, *Life Without Father* (New York: Free Press, 1996), 14.

**Chapter 6.   Father—Values Sorter**

1. Stanley Coopersmith, *The Antecedents of Self Esteem* (San Francisco: W. H. Freeman and Company, 1967).

2. *Webster's New World Dictionary,* college ed. (Cleveland and New York: World Publishing Co., 1957).

3. Coopersmith, *The Antecedents of Self Esteem.*

**Other References**

1. Nick Stinnett and John DeFrain, *The Six Secrets of Strong Families* (Boston and Toronto: Little, Brown and Company, 1985).

2. Ken Canfield, *The Heart of a Father: How Dads Can Shape the Destiny of America* (Chicago: Northfield Publishing, 1996).

3. Richard Louv, *Father Love, What We Need, What We Seek, What We Must Create* (New York: Pocket Books, 1993).